LIGHT
from
AFAR

AN ADVENT DEVOTIONAL
FROM AROUND THE WORLD

UPPER
ROOM BOOKS®
NASHVILLE

LIGHT FROM AFAR: An Advent Devotional from Around the World
Copyright © 2023 by Upper Room Books*
All rights reserved.

No part of this book may be reproduced in any manner whatsoever without permission except for brief quotations in critical articles or reviews. For information, write Upper Room Books®, 1908 Grand Avenue, Nashville, TN 37212.

Upper Room Books® website: upperroombooks.com

Upper Room®, Upper Room Books®, and design logos are trademarks owned by The Upper Room®, Nashville, Tennessee. All rights reserved.

Scripture quotations are from the New Revised Standard Version Updated Edition. Copyright © 2021 National Council of Churches of Christ in the United States of America. Used by permission. All rights reserved worldwide.

At the time of publication, all websites referenced in this book were valid. However, due to the fluid nature of the Internet, some addresses may have changed or the content may no longer be relevant.

Cover design: LUCAS Art & Design
Interior design and typesetting: PerfecType | Nashville, TN

Print ISBN: 978-0-8358-2037-0
Epub ISBN: 978-0-8358-2038-7

Printed in the United States of America

CONTENTS

INTRODUCTION

In the time of King Herod, after Jesus was born in
Bethlehem of Judea, magi from the east came to
Jerusalem, asking, "Where is the child who has been
born king of the Jews? For we observed his star in
the east and have come to pay him homage."

Matthew 2:1-2

Welcome to *Light from Afar: An Advent Devotional from Around the World*. As those magi from long ago followed a light in the sky to guide them on their pilgrimage to find the Holy Child, so we, as followers of Christ, are making this pilgrimage once again, with light-bearers from four different countries as our guides.

Whether a journey to Jerusalem, the Island of Iona in Scotland, or the Camino de Santiago in northwestern Spain, pilgrims for centuries have made these kinds of *outer journeys that allow for an inner transformation.* We are on such a journey now, as we make our way to the birth of the Christ Child.

This Advent pilgrimage will take us on a journey through four countries: Brazil, the Philippines, Ukraine, and South Africa. Four thoughtful Christian guides help us to reflect on Advent and Christmas in their countries by bringing wisdom, courage, and colorful anecdotes to each scripture selection:

Cláudio Carvalhaes, a native Brazilian theologian, brings light from Brazil and from his childhood growing up in the global South.

Joel Bengbeng is a district superintendent of The United Methodist Church in the Philippines who brings a challenging, prophetic approach to the Advent scriptures, using examples from his country's own history.

Nadiyka Gerbish is a Ukrainian writer and podcaster. Her reflections are ripped from the headlines of the war in Ukraine, giving rare glimpses of what life as a faithful Christian in wartime Advent looks like.

Sidwell Mokgothu is a bishop in the Methodist Church of Southern Africa and brings the full weight of South African history and culture to bear on his interpretation and reflections on Advent scripture.

Pilgrims of old prepared themselves for the journey ahead through ritual, rhythm, and spiritual practice. Here are some reminders for this Advent pilgrimage:

Daily spiritual practice is important. Nourish yourself each day by reading the suggested scripture passage and the meditation. Take time for the three-step conclusion of each meditation:

* *Pray.* A written prayer is suggested for you to read. Pause and add your own impromptu prayers.
* *Reflect.* Read the question for reflection. Pause to think about the question. Write your thoughts in response in your journal. Carry the question in your heart during the day.
* *Listen.* Each day's meditation has an accompanying music video, found at https://UpperRoomBooks.com/LightFromAfar or by using the QR code at the right. Each day, access the link given for a song from that country. Allow yourself time to enjoy music you may not recognize and notice how it affects you and draws you closer to God. Be open to what you may learn from another culture.

Companions along the way are essential. Gather with others to discuss this book, and meet together each week of Advent. We need one another for comfort, support, and encouragement. A small-group guide for using this book is included on page 95.

Be present to the present. Let this daily practice keep you from rushing through Advent, swept up in the consumerist pressure of the season in our culture. Allow this prayer time to ground you in holy space as you make your way to Christmas Day. Notice the ways in which you are looking at daily life differently as a result of your time in scripture and prayer. Be alert to holy moments.

Stay curious. Being on pilgrimage or even just traveling to another country means encountering new information, new people, and new experiences. What can you learn from the lives of these international guides that you wouldn't have known before?

Using this Book

The readings and exercises in this book are designed for daily use throughout the season of Advent, beginning on the first Sunday of Advent and ending on or around Christmas Day. There are meditations for all seven days of the week for each of the four weeks of Advent. Allow ten to fifteen minutes to complete the reading and prayer.

Find a quiet place where you can read and pray with this book each day. Finding this time and place may not be easy in the hurried days leading up to Christmas, but your Advent journey will be the better for it.

Materials Needed

All you need to follow this resource is a personal copy of *Light from Afar*, a Bible, and something to write in, such as a journal or notebook. Some people find it helpful to light a candle before beginning to read.

Have your phone or computer nearby to listen to the suggested song for each day. The music in this resource is an additional sensory component that will add much to your devotional experience. Be sure to allow time for this prayerful listening.

Now, let us begin. Grab a walking stick, your Bible, and a few friends. The pilgrimage awaits.

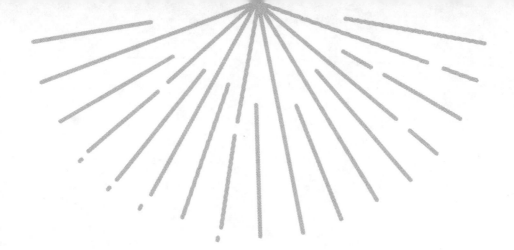

FIRST WEEK OF ADVENT

Light from Brazil

Hope

Cláudio Carvalhaes

Bearers of Light

READ | James 1:16-18

Every generous act of giving, with every perfect gift, is from above, coming down from the Father of lights, with whom there is no variation or shadow due to change.

James 1:17

I love the title of this Advent study—*Light from Afar*. We all carry a light within us, a light God has placed in us when we were made in God's image. This light illumines and warms our path like a fire through our days. It is our task to keep this light shining. Just as the song says: "This little light of mine, I'm gonna let it shine!" Advent is about light, God's light to the world. The star in the sky guiding the three magi was already God's light to the world. That light, back then, from afar, is the light that shines in our hearts today. When I search for my own light during this season, I see that the light that shines within me is also a light that comes from afar. The light within me takes me back to that manger where Jesus was born as a refugee, hiding from a tyrant who was killing small children. The light of the fire that warmed Joseph, Mary, Jesus, and the animals is the same light that warms my heart when I feel cold.

I also have to go back to where I was born and see that the light that now shines on me comes from the South, from São Paulo, Brazil. When I was born, it was not an easy time for my family. My father had had an accident and couldn't work. My mother was already working by herself to sustain three kids. And now an unexpected child was arriving. Somehow, they made a way out of no way. The light within my mother and my father, a light given from God, was the light that shone within me. They were able to make it because there was a small Presbyterian church that gave me everything I needed: toys, food, stories, songs. That community was the light that kept my body warm and my spirit alive, shining like the sun at midday. I give thanks for the grace of God given to me through this beautiful community.

We are all the result of a cosmic light: the light of God who created the pluriverses and shines on the stars was the light that shone on Jesus and keeps shining through the work of the Holy Spirit everywhere. That cosmic light shone in the lives of my mother, father, and siblings and on the folks of that small Presbyterian congregation in São Paulo. As we move through these Advent weeks, I would like to ask you to inquire about your own light. Where does your light come from?

Advent is the preparation for the light of God to come. Advent is a time when we light our path so the gospel of Jesus can be fully lived, reminding us of the ways of the light of God within us. For the light to exist, it is necessary to have darkness. And our God is both light and darkness. The darkness of God is both the manifestation of God's presence and the latent forms of God's light within us. Embracing darkness, we will celebrate the light of Jesus coming to us during this Advent. I will bring a light from afar: the light from the South of the American continent. Shall we be lights for one another on this journey?

PRAY | God of Light, illumine our darkness and fill us with expectation for the coming of your son. We are on this journey with you. Amen.

REFLECT | Who were the people whose light shone on your life and gave you warmth? How did the light of God keep you going this far?

LISTEN | "Momento Novo" by Viva Vida and Gente da Casa

Advent in Brazil

READ | 1 Corinthians 1:3-9

> *I give thanks to my God always for you because of the*
> *grace of God that has been given you in Christ Jesus, for in*
> *every way you have been enriched in him, in speech and*
> *knowledge of every kind—just as the testimony of Christ has*
> *been strengthened among you—so that you are not lacking*
> *in any gift as you wait for the revealing of our Lord Jesus*
> *Christ. He will also strengthen you to the end, so that you*
> *may be blameless on the day of our Lord Jesus Christ. God is*
> *faithful, by whom you were called into the partnership of his*
> *Son, Jesus Christ our Lord.*
>
> 1 Corinthians 1:4-9

I grew up in São Paulo, Brazil. My little church was a joyful community. There was always laughter and playfulness and games. Every summer, we would play all kinds of games, from ping-pong to soccer. The church was my playground.

Liturgically, Advent wasn't celebrated that much in my church, but there was a feeling of joy that would take us over before Christmas. We would celebrate together with delicious meals and some gifts. The church always provided gifts for us kids, and that would offset the fear of not getting anything at home. The church would put up lights and a little tree. The whole assembly would live in a state of happiness that was so reassuring of life itself.

In Brazil, we have an expression about happiness: "Happiness is the proof of the nine." That expression doesn't have anything to do with a mathematics proof but rather with the sense that happiness is the most important thing in life. Joy is what makes life real and true. If you have happiness, joy, and laughter, you are alive.

Brazil has samba, soccer, celebrations, and festivities everywhere. It is a very joyful culture. The Brazilian theologian Rubem Alves used to say that we do not rely on the utility of life but on the fruition of life. He said, "Poetry, music, painting, sculpture, dance, theater, cooking: they are all games we invent so that the body finds happiness, even if in brief moments of distraction." So now during Advent, I make a special point of finding the joy in my life and community.

PRAY | God of laughter, fun, games, dance, joy, and happiness, we have Jesus as joy to the world and to our lives. May we learn to never let joy go. For if we lose joy, we lose Jesus. In Jesus' name, we pray. Amen.

REFLECT | How are you making a point of finding joy in your life during Advent? What in your life makes happiness "the proof of the nine"?

LISTEN | "Xote da Vitória" by Viva Vida and Gente da Casa

Collective, Active Hope

READ | Psalm 80:1-7, 17-19

Restore us, O God;
let your face shine, that we may be saved.

O LORD God of hosts,
how long will you be angry with your people's prayers?
You have fed them with the bread of tears
and given them tears to drink in full measure.
You make us the scorn of our neighbors;
our enemies laugh among themselves.

Restore us, O God of hosts;
let your face shine, that we may be saved.

Psalm 80:3-7

When my mother gave birth to me, everything was uncertain. Our household was financially broken and seemingly little could be done. The church we attended restored the soul of our family. That little church was the advent of hope for our family. By giving us concrete hope for our very bodies, this church brought us spiritual hope. There is no way we can separate the cultural, political, economic, ecological, and religious aspects of our faith.

It was there that I learned that hope is not specific to an individual but held by a whole community. In Latin America, the invitation to pray to God for restoration is an act of collective hope. The hope lies in the path of liberation for all those who are poor, lonely, disrespected, destroyed, misunderstood, put down, killed.

At this time of Advent, we hope and we pray that God's light will shine upon those who are suffering, those who do not have enough to eat, those who are afraid, those who are in prison, those who are in pain. We ask God's light to shine upon the animals, the rivers, and the mountains. We ask for the sick to be healed, the broken to be made whole, the hungry to be fed, the broken and dismantled to be restored, our families to be visited by the Spirit, our politics to be transformed, our trees to be protected, our rivers to be clean, our animals to be respected, our culture to show signs of happiness, and that we will all be saved.

PRAY | God of hosts, we long for you. Our hopes lie in you, who have empowered us to act on this hope and made your kin-dom present on earth. Restore in us the active hope that changes things everywhere. May you restore in us the hope we have lost. May your face rekindle in us the light we have lost along the way. May your salvation come to the whole world: people, animals, seas, mountains, and the whole earth. Amen.

REFLECT | Today, what are your deepest forms of hope? What prayers of restoration do you need to pray today?

LISTEN | "Louvor" by Viva Vida and Gente da Casa

Gathered in Arms of Love

READ | Isaiah 40:1-11

> *Comfort, O comfort my people,*
> *   says your God.*
> *Speak tenderly to Jerusalem,*
> *   and cry to her*
> *that she has served her term,*
> *   that her penalty is paid,*
> *that she has received from the LORD's hand*
> *   double for all her sins.*
> *He will feed his flock like a shepherd;*
> *   he will gather the lambs in his arms*
> *and carry them in his bosom*
> *   and gently lead the mother sheep.*
>
> Isaiah 40:1-2, 11

Oppression in Latin American history is pervasive. Since colonization, forces of death have massacred native people and Black people and pushed so many people to live in abject poverty. While my church never talked about these forms of death in our society, I knew that I was sheltered in a community of people who loved me. There were the older women who kept the church going. There were the women leading Sunday school for us kids, and that was the best time of my life. The church gave me songs, stories, socialization, and a way in the world.

When I pursued higher education, that church supported me. I never felt alone in society because my church was my most important community. From there, I learned to love the world I lived in. Every Sunday, I was showered with love by Ms. Eny, Maria, Eliana, and so many other people. My pastors loved my family, and I *felt* loved. We were comforted every Sunday with the loving gospel of Jesus Christ. Because of that, I also learned I had to comfort God's people. The love I received was transformed into a mission to love the world. Just as "God so loved the world that he gave his only Son" (John 3:16), I had the mission to show this love to the world. Love begets love.

When Advent came, I felt my heart infused with a love I knew about! Love was everywhere. I had so much anticipation for Christmas simply because there was so much love around me.

PRAY | God of love, teach us to love the world as you love us. Teach us to love beyond limits and through complications. It is so hard to truly love. Teach us that true love you have for us so we can show the world who you are: True Love. Amen.

REFLECT | What people or groups of people in your life have laid a foundation of love for you in such a way as to allow you to be able to experience Advent love more fully? Give thanks for these people.

LISTEN | "Coração de um povo" by Viva Vida and Gente da Casa

Peace and Justice for the Earth

READ | Jeremiah 33:14-16

> *The days are surely coming, says the LORD, when I will fulfill the promise I made to the house of Israel and the house of Judah. In those days and at that time I will cause a righteous Branch to spring up for David, and he shall execute justice and righteousness in the land.*
>
> Jeremiah 33:14-15

Martin Luther King Jr. taught us that there is no peace without justice. There is no peace when life is burning, being destroyed, broken apart. During this Advent, we need to think of peace not only for human beings but for animals and the earth as well. Animals need to live in peace; forests need to live in peace; oceans need to live in peace. That means that animals, forests, and oceans need justice. But what exactly does that mean?

I believe that unless we care deeply for the earth, we cannot live in peace. There is no peace without justice for the earth. John 3:16 says that "God so loved the *world*." Now, we must understand this passage differently from how we have been used to understanding it. This verse includes God's love for more than humans; the apostle John didn't say "For God so loved *humans*. . . ." This means that even all that is not human is also deeply loved by God. From the worms who cultivate the land to the bees and the eagles, birds and foxes, beavers and dolphins, sharks, cats, dogs and so on, God loves every being!

Moreover, God so loved the rivers, the mountains, the plants, the clouds, the winds, the fire, and everything that this earth is made of. *Everything* was and is so loved by God.

This Advent, peace for the earth itself should be at the heart of our prayers, concerns, thanksgivings, and celebrations. "Peace on earth" is more—way more—than a human endeavor. We must join our actions with God's desire to keep forests and rivers and animals alive, even in the midst of climate catastrophe. We believe that the peace that Jesus brings to us during Advent is paired with justice for all the earth.

PRAY | God of all creation, we are grateful for every single living being on this precious planet. Everything is so alive and everything deserves peace. May Jesus, the Prince of Peace, help us bring peace and justice to your whole creation. Amen.

REFLECT | Is the idea that "God so loved" all the earth a new perspective for you? How can you join your love for a certain part of creation with God's love, through action?

LISTEN | "Pequenos" by Viva Vida and Gente da Casa

God's Love for the Whole Earth

READ | Psalm 89:1-4, 19-26

> *I will sing of your steadfast love, O LORD, forever;*
> > *with my mouth I will proclaim your faithfulness to all*
> > *generations.*
> *I declare that your steadfast love is established forever;*
> > *your faithfulness is as firm as the heavens.*

Psalm 89:1-2

To experience Advent from the viewpoint of the earth that God loves, we have to change our point of view. For example, if I were to transport myself back to Latin America and land in the Amazon rainforest, what would Advent mean there? How can I find God's steadfast love there?

From my perspective, unless we fight for the forests, rivers, oceans, and animals to survive, we will not have the opportunity to continue celebrating Jesus on the earth. The life of the earth must guide our questions. Perhaps we could focus on the animals at the manger: oxen, donkeys, cows, sheep. So many species are in danger of extinction. If we consider the animals today as central to our Advent stories, what would hope, peace, joy, and love look like?

We cannot have joy without the plurality of species on earth. Hope for humanity is only possible if there are habitats for all animals to coexist, not just humans. What does God have to do with forests, rivers, and the fullness of life within ecosystems? God's steadfast love is not only for human beings but for the whole earth.

PRAY | God of all beings, as we prepare for the coming of Jesus, help us not forget the animals who were Jesus' companions at his birth. May we orient our faith toward the protection of all species during this Advent, and may we learn to live with them not through fear but with hope, peace, joy, and love. Amen.

REFLECT | What if to love God is to love animals? Where do you see this kind of love in your life?

LISTEN | "Na visão dos novos profetas" by Viva Vida and Gente da Casa

Awake and Ready for Advent

READ | Mark 13:24-37

Therefore, keep awake, for you do not know when the master of the house will come, in the evening or at midnight or at cockcrow or at dawn, or else he may find you asleep when he comes suddenly. And what I say to you I say to all: Keep awake.

Mark 13:35-37

During Advent, we must keep awake to our four Advent themes: hope, peace, joy, and love, and ask ourselves: "What is our joy during these days? What do we hope for during Advent that will follow us through the whole new year? Whom do we love or need to love, starting now? What kind of peace are we talking about during the preparation for Jesus' birth?"

During this time of Advent, our strength is reawakened in many unfolding ways. The Spirit of God is at work to renew our hope, peace, joy, and love. The light inside will be lit again and our spiritual fire rekindled. It is the constancy of the life of Jesus in us that helps us renew our vows to love one another, to act in hope for transformation, to act in hope for the healing of our communities and the world, and to pray about bringing peace to the earth.

Each week of Advent, we are called back to these four ideas, which are also four feelings. Time and again, we must awaken to these questions in light of Advent so that when Christmas comes, we have a better sense of what Jesus' birth is all about and what the invitations are for us, if we are to follow that little child. From the South, I am always reminded of the poor, of those who cannot afford shelter, health care, warmth, and food. From the South, I am reminded to have hope, peace, joy, and love as I live with others who are not like me and all beings that need my deep care and the fullness of my faith.

PRAY | God of promises, we expect your coming with the fullness of our hearts. Help us orient our life toward your whole creation. Help us learn how to live in hope, peace, joy, and love with one another. Amen.

REFLECT | In that ways can you learn to love God in more expansive ways? Are you awake and ready for these challenges again this Advent?

LISTEN | "Mesmo porque . . ." by Viva Vida and Gente da Casa

SECOND WEEK OF ADVENT

Light from the Philippines

Peace

Joel Bengbeng

Advent and Christmas in the Philippines

READ | Psalm 27:1-14

> *The LORD is my light and my salvation;*
> *whom shall I fear?*
> *The LORD is the stronghold of my life;*
> *of whom shall I be afraid?*

Psalm 27:1

Advent as a liturgical celebration is relatively new in the faith community where I grew up. It is said that our country, the Philippines, has the longest Christmas season in the world. As early as September, when the climate gets cooler, Christmas songs are played in public vehicles, homes, and shopping malls. Perhaps Christmas begins too early, but unfortunately, it also ends too soon. After Christmas Day, one rarely hears Christmas music, and churches stop singing Christmas songs.

In our country, the days before Christmas are part of the yearly holiday break. During my childhood days, that period was spent on daily rehearsals for our church's Christmas celebration. Each child would be given a scripture verse to be recited before the entire congregation. Christmas carols, acrostics, tableau, and poems were rehearsed as well. After church rehearsals, children would form groups and move from one house to another, singing Christmas carols. In return, households would give them money.

Church and civic organizations would also use this season to raise funds for different programs and ministries.

In more recent times, our Advent liturgical celebration has been shaped and influenced by Roman Catholicism. Churches have adapted the Roman Catholic nine-day daily Mass preceding Christmas Day called *Simbang Gabi*. Filipino Catholics celebrate this as a Marian *novena* (ninth, recitation of prayers over nine days) in honor of Mary's role in the conception and birth of the Savior. Masses are held either in the evening (*Misa de Aguinaldo* or "gift or special Mass") or at dawn (*Misa de Gallo* or "Mass of the Rooster"), so that the farmers and workers can participate without sacrificing their jobs. This practice has also been embraced by United Methodist congregations in the country. Every morning or evening, people flock to the churches, bringing with them their special prayer petitions. Many believe that attending all nine services will result in answered prayers. Laypersons take turns preaching. Families or small groups are assigned to lead services and provide refreshments or meals following the service. Church members who do not show up on ordinary Sundays come at least once during Simbang Gabi and on Christmas Eve. In the district where I serve as a superintendent, Eucharist or Holy Communion has been an essential part of our daily services. These nine-day services have changed the spiritual and social landscape of many United Methodists ever since. The services have created a deeper sense of excitement, expectation, and anticipation for the coming Christmas Day.

PRAY | Gracious God, may our Advent days be filled with prayers and worship so that we keep our hearts focused on the coming Christ. Amen.

REFLECT | What practice from another church or denomination could you try this Advent to bring new life to your experience? Look around your community for possibilities.

LISTEN | "Ang Puso Ko'y Nagpupuri" ("My Heart Praises the Lord") by Bukas Palad Ministry

Radical Good News

READ | Mark 1:1-8

> *So John the baptizer appeared in the wilderness, proclaiming*
> *a baptism of repentance for the forgiveness of sins. He*
> *proclaimed, "The one who is more powerful than I is coming*
> *after me; I am not worthy to stoop down and untie the strap*
> *of his sandals. I have baptized you with water, but he will*
> *baptize you with the Holy Spirit."*
>
> Mark 1:4, 7-8

Each liturgical year begins with the season of Advent. This season marks a new start in the church's yearlong journey with Christ. Too often for us, Advent, Christmas, and the gospel in general have lost their radical character. The story of Christ's birth has been relegated to a Disneyland-like, sugar-coated story devoid of political and social implications, focused exclusively in welcoming Christ as "personal Lord and Savior."

"The beginning of the good news of Jesus Christ, the Son of God" (Mark 1:1). This first verse of Mark's Gospel does not contain a main verb. It's more like a book title or a news headline. Mark's writing contains stories, parables, exorcisms, teachings, and narratives as the beginning of the good news of the Messiah.

The Greek word for "good news" is *evangelion*. It was not a strictly religious term in the Roman Empire. It was used by the Roman military to announce a victory in war, to proclaim the arrival of the emperor, or to declare that a new territory was conquered. In employing this word to describe the coming of Jesus as well as to his life and ministry, Mark and the early Christians were doing something dangerous: They were asserting that Jesus is the Son of God, not the emperor who claimed this title for himself. They were telling the world that Jesus' coming, life, and teachings were the true *evangelion,* not the arrival of the emperor. According to Mark, Jesus Christ is the crucified and risen Lord, the fulfillment of God's kingdom breaking into the life of the world and challenging all human authorities who play God.

As we go through the first several chapters in Mark, we read that crowds were following Jesus because of his growing authority and influence. Jesus was slowly becoming a growing threat to the occupying authorities of the Roman Empire. Every story of healing or forgiveness in the first half of Mark is in direct defiance of some political or religious power. All human powers are subject to the authority of God, an authority characterized by mercy, a revolutionary rule of love focused on the vulnerable. Jesus is the Son of God who liberates God's people—from tyranny, from those who use and abuse authority to systematically harm the poor, and from religious leadership and ideology that take advantage of the weak.

From "the beginning," John the Baptist leads us in this Advent season to our true Lord, whose birth we await and whose reign is eternal. However, God's liberating acts do not end in Mark's Gospel. The story begins with Jesus. But it goes on and on. As a baptized community, this new beginning takes place in our hearing or reading of this *evangelion.* This good news breaks into our own lives the moment we pledge allegiance to Jesus as the Son of God. As Jesus said, we can continue the work he started.

PRAY | Liberating God, your love gives us the courage, vision, and conviction to reject, resist, and renounce evil, injustice, and oppression in all forms. May we continue your work on earth. Amen.

REFLECT | In what ways have you believed in a "sugar-coated story devoid of political and social implications"? How does a clear reading of the Gospels change that perspective?

LISTEN | "Humayo't' Ihayag" ("Go Forth and Reveal") by Bukas Palad Music Ministry

Signs of Hope

READ | Isaiah 11:1-10

> *A shoot shall come out from the stump of Jesse,*
>   *and a branch shall grow out of his roots.*
> *The wolf shall live with the lamb;*
>   *the leopard shall lie down with the kid;*
> *the calf and the lion will feed together,*
>   *and a little child shall lead them.*

Isaiah 11:1, 6

Today's reading is presented in the context of the Syro-Ephraimite conflict in which Syria and the Northern Kingdom (Israel) join forces against the Southern Kingdom of Judah. In the midst of chaos, war, and destruction, a green shoot will sprout from a dead stump to establish a kingdom of justice and peace. God gave Isaiah a vision of shalom, a new creation brought about by the coming of a messianic ruler. This vision also echoes the harmony of the Garden of Eden or the first creation. In his *Notes on the New Testament*, John Wesley interprets verses 6-8 literally and figuratively: "The creatures shall be restored to that state of innocency in which they were before the fall of man. Men of fierce, and cruel dispositions, shall be so transformed by the grace of Christ, that they shall become gentle, and tractable."

All around us, the poor continue to suffer injustice and discrimination. An ordinary offender is immediately punished, while those who hold power are acquitted in the blink of an eye. But in God's new or renewed creation, peace is rooted in and intertwined with justice or righteousness. There will be no peace without justice. It is only when justice thrives that the poor, lowly, humble, powerless, vulnerable, and weak are safe in the hands of those who hold power. No more predators and victims.

A fresh shoot will sprout out of a dead stump. Life springs out of death and desolation. No matter how the present condition pales in comparison with what God intends, that vision has a transformative character. It shapes the way we look at our own lives, the way we regard one another and the world around us right here, right now. There's still a huge amount of work to do, both in the church and in the world. This is true not only in the life of the world but in our own lives as well. No matter how broken we think we are, or how many times we think we are beyond repair, surely there are signs of hope and new beginnings. In the face of sin and among the stumps of our own lives, we cling to the vision of the way God created things to be. God loves repairing broken lives and restoring destroyed communities.

We only need to learn to see and appreciate small glimpses of peace and love right in our midst. At our Eucharistic tables, we catch glimpses of wolves eating with lambs. At our worship services, we see images of leopards coexisting with goats. In faith communities where some are pushed to the peripheries, we see hope among individuals who see God's image in every person.

PRAY | Loving God, you demonstrated your love through coming to us as a small, defenseless infant, a sign that you will fulfill your covenantal promise to inaugurate a new creation where peace and justice will reign. May we be a part of your active love. Amen.

REFLECT | Where do you see glimpses of God's new creation coming to pass around you?

LISTEN | "Dakilang Katapatan" ("Great Loyalty") by Papuri Singers

John's Subversive Baptism

READ | Luke 3:1-6

> *[John] went into all the region around the Jordan,*
> *proclaiming a baptism of repentance for the forgiveness of*
> *sins, as it is written in the book of the words of the prophet*
> *Isaiah,*
>
> *"The voice of one crying out in the wilderness:*
> *'Prepare the way of the Lord;*
> *make his paths straight.'"*
>
> Luke 3:3-4

Year after year, readings about John the Baptist occupy two Sundays during the Advent season. In our reading today, Luke quotes Isaiah 40:3. The passage is part of the oracle of comfort, referring to the return of the exiled Israelites in Babylon around 538 BCE. As the Lord led the enslaved Hebrews by way of the desert into the Promised Land in the Exodus story, now the Lord is leading his people out of the Babylonian exile back to Jerusalem. In employing the two important events in the life of Israel (freedom from slavery in Egypt and from Babylonian exile), Luke understands John's role as a messenger who announces the advent of a Savior who will lead a "new exodus" and liberate God's people from slavery and captivity. John went into all the country around the Jordan River, proclaiming a baptism of repentance for the forgiveness of sins. He then led penitents to the Jordan River for the ritual of baptism, anticipating the coming of the Messiah.

All these events happened in a specific religious, social, and political context, which Luke vividly describes in the first two verses of chapter 3. God entered in a certain period of time and history. The first followers of Christ did not live in a social and political vacuum. They were subjects of a tyrannical empire that conquered nations. That is why Luke bothered to list the names of the ruling political and religious figures during those days. Tiberius, Pilate, and Herod were noted. The high priests Annas and Caiaphas are mentioned as well. Both John and Jesus ministered in the context of a definite hierarchical political structure that dominated and oppressed people. These religious leaders were indebted to the political rulers for their positions, because at that time, the high priest was appointed or reappointed annually by the Roman authority. Hence, John ministered right in the middle of a realm defined by political and religious leaders. John summoned the people to return to the Lord. It was a call to leave Egypt and Babylon and cross to the other side.

This redirection of lives toward God is expressed and sealed through the baptism of repentance. While John's baptism is not a Christian baptism, this Advent passage invites us to look at the revolutionary character of the sacrament of baptism. We cannot ignore the social and, therefore, political implications of baptism. Baptism is a renunciation of allegiances to any human authority, submission to God's authority alone, and alignment of oneself to the coming kingdom. Unlike the high priests, John's extraordinary authority was not derived from the political powers of his day. In fact, it was an illegitimate, and therefore, subversive authority. He did not benefit from the status quo and the ruling regime. Baptism, therefore, marks allegiance to a different kingdom and a new authority. This new status might have cost the lives of those who chose to follow the one whom John the Baptist proclaimed.

We cannot celebrate Christmas without going through Advent first. We cannot welcome the Christ Child if we do not listen to John the Baptist first. If we take seriously the message of John the Baptist, Christmas will surely have a new and deeper significance this year.

PRAY | Gracious God, we align ourselves with you, your ways, and your authority. May we be reminded that we belong to your reign, even as we live in our specific time and place. Amen.

REFLECT | Today, remember your baptism. How do you understand it as a subversive act?

LISTEN | "Be Not Afraid—Himig Heswita" sung by Oggie Benipayo

Love Drives Out Darkness

READ | Luke 1:68-79

> *Because of the tender mercy of our God,*
> *the dawn from on high will break upon us,*
> *to shine upon those who sit in darkness and in the shadow of*
> *death,*
> *to guide our feet into the way of peace.*
>
> Luke 1:78-79

Some argue that darkness isn't something that exists, but simply a phenomenon used to describe the absence of something. Unlike light, which is made of very small packets of electromagnetic energy called photons (the smallest unit of radiant energy), darkness is made of nothing. It is simply the absence of light.

The season of Advent covers December 21, which is the longest night in the Northern Hemisphere. During this season, the days become shorter and the nights longer. But darkness is more than a physical reality. We go through spiritual darkness every day of our lives. Having suffered depression, I know what it is like to be in the dark: losing your self-esteem, struggling to find reasons to get up every morning, having a hard time finding meaning in things you used to enjoy, constantly worrying what might go wrong, and entertaining thoughts of ending your life. But even in those darkest moments of my life, I was confident of God's constant presence, whether I was aware of it or not.

The Song of Zechariah, also known as the "Benedictus," was Zechariah's first words following the birth of his son, John the Baptist, after several months of being mute. His song describes his profound joy at seeing the unfolding of God's promises for God's people. God fulfills God's promises no matter what. God comes to help God's people and set them free and rescue them from death, like "the dawn from on high" to shine on those living in darkness, fear, oppression, and death. Zechariah speaks in the present tense, as if God has already done what God intends to do. In God's coming through Jesus Christ, God has pierced the darkness. Advent celebrates and proclaims Christ's three comings: his birth, his daily presence, and his second coming. Therefore, as we prepare to celebrate Christ's first coming, we also celebrate evidences of his daily coming right here, right now, and we eagerly anticipate his coming again.

Daily, we witness or experience the reality of darkness in this world. The mission of the church is to reflect and offer Christ as the light of the world so that darkness might be overcome. If darkness is the absence of light, the darkness in the world is the absence of God's people being bearers of Christ's light in the world. It's the result of our failure to radiate and reflect the love of God. Madeleine L'Engle said, "Maybe you have to know the darkness before you can appreciate the light" (*A Ring of Endless Light*). Never lose hope; the darkest moment is a sign that the dawn is near.

PRAY | God of light and love, your light always wins over darkness. Give us eyes to search for the light, even when it seems that the darkness may overcome us. Amen.

REFLECT | Ponder the Madeleine L'Engle quote: "Maybe you have to know the darkness before you can appreciate the light." How have you experienced this in your life?

LISTEN | "Halina, Emmanuel" (Come, Emmanuel) by DIADEMS Virtual Choir

Good News to the Poor

READ | Psalm 72:1-7, 18-19

> *Give the king your justice, O God,*
> *and your righteousness to a king's son.*
> *May he judge your people with righteousness*
> *and your poor with justice.*
> *May the mountains yield prosperity for the people,*
> *and the hills, in righteousness.*
> *May he defend the cause of the poor of the people,*
> *give deliverance to the needy,*
> *and crush the oppressor.*
>
> Psalm 72:1-4

Writing these series of reflections has helped me appreciate and see clearly the wider meaning of Advent, especially its political implications, which is often ignored in the popular expressions of Advent and Christmas spirituality. Christians are often divided in their views about their relationship with the state and political leaders. In much of its history, Christianity has aligned itself with political figures, often becoming the state's tool rather than its conscience. On the other hand, some traditions totally reject the state and adhere to the doctrine of theocracy.

Today's psalm starts with a plea to God to teach the king with God's righteousness and share with him God's own justice, so that he will rule and govern justly (verses 1 and 2). This plea reappears in verse 4. The king is expected to "defend" the cause of the poor and the needy, while destroying their oppressor. The king's success and victory lies in his compassion and care for the needy, the poor, the helpless, and the oppressed. Like the entirety of the Old Testament witness, this psalm reflects God's special attention to the marginalized. God is the God of all, but God identifies particularly with the *anawim*—a Hebrew word for the poor and the oppressed who depend on God for deliverance. The king, being God's regent, is expected to use his power to empower the powerless and defend those who cannot defend themselves.

The ultimate litmus test of leadership is how those entrusted with such power treat others, especially the poorest. The barometer of a nation's righteousness is how it treats the most vulnerable in its midst. Any leadership or authority that tramples upon the poor is contrary to God's will. Taking care of the poor, however, goes beyond electing leaders with integrity. It requires dismantling the systems that oppress them. It means moving from compassion for the poor to advocating justice for the poor.

Jesus' parables, teachings, miracles, and narrative stories portray Jesus as the Messiah who embodies the righteous rule of a king:

> The Spirit of the Lord is upon me,
>> because he has anointed me
>>> to bring good news to the poor.
> He has sent me to proclaim release to the captives
>> and recovery of sight to the blind,
>>> to set free those who are oppressed. (Luke 4:18)

PRAY | Righteous God, help us to hold our political leaders accountable to extending your justice and righteousness to the needy, especially during this season of Advent. Amen.

REFLECT | The author writes, "The barometer of a nation's righteousness is how it treats the most vulnerable in its midst." How do you rate your country's righteousness against this statement? What is your prayer for your country in this regard?

LISTEN | "Misyon" by Gary Granada

Seeing Christ in the Other

READ | Romans 15:4-13

> *May the God of steadfastness and encouragement grant you*
> *to live in harmony with one another, in accordance with*
> *Christ Jesus, so that together you may with one voice glorify*
> *the God and Father of our Lord Jesus Christ. Welcome one*
> *another, therefore, just as Christ has welcomed you, for the*
> *glory of God.*
>
> Romans 15:5-7

The Philippines is one of the most culturally, linguistically, and ethnically diverse countries in the world. It has more than 175 ethnolinguistic groups scattered in about 2,000 islands. Our diversity makes us a beautiful people, but many times it causes painful divisions. Spanish colonizers took advantage of these divisions, employing divide-and-conquer tactics to easily subjugate our ancestors. They created animosity among different cultural groups.

Scholars agree that the house churches in Rome were diverse communities composed of Jews and Gentiles. Paul admonished them to "Welcome one another, . . . as Christ has welcomed you." Imagine the historically divided races breaking bread and sharing a common cup at one table together! Paul underscores the Hebrew Scripture prophesying that the Gentiles must join their praises to the children of Israel (see Romans 15:10-12).

The expression of God's grace is manifested in Jews and Gentiles living and worshiping together. The Paschal Mystery—Christ's passion, death, and resurrection for the salvation of Jews and Gentiles—shows the nature of God's grace: it is a gift given without consideration of worldly wealth or status. The grace of God for all people overcomes the divisions within the Christian community.

Unity according to Christ does not mean that differences are eradicated. The essential and defining character of identity is Jesus Christ himself. Our call is to radiate Christ together in the midst of our diversity. Our faith demands rejecting the human-made boundaries of culture, ethnicity, gender, or economic status, becoming one household under the same roof, giving room for those who are different from us. Do we see Paul's command realized in our respective communities? Or do we keep redefining "welcome" to fit our narrow understanding of love?

Some argue that welcoming all kinds of people would make God's grace cheap. How could God's grace be cheap if it is all-encompassing? Perhaps it becomes cheap if we make it exclusive and divisive. But grace is grace. It is never cheap. Otherwise, it is not grace. God's light will never completely shine in the world unless we better reflect the story of radical love—the story of Jesus Christ who has accepted all into God's family.

We will never reach our full identity in Christ until we see Christ in the face of the other. Advent is not simply preparation for Christmas. Instead, we are making ourselves ready to meet Christ in the most unexpected people, including those who do not belong to the circle that we created to exclude others.

PRAY | God of diversity, help us to welcome the stranger, sit next to someone who does not look like us, and eat with those who think differently than we do. May your grace be offered to all, through us, this Advent. Amen.

REFLECT | When the gospel is used to justify marginalization, discrimination, bigotry, and hatred toward the other, our hope diminishes and our Advent light dims. What acts brighten the light of Advent?

LISTEN | "Pananagutan" by Bugoy Drilon

THIRD WEEK OF ADVENT

Light from Ukraine

Joy

Nadiyka Gerbish

Advent and Christmas in Ukraine

READ | John 8:12-20

> *Again Jesus spoke to them, saying, "I am the light of the*
> *world. Whoever follows me will never walk in darkness but*
> *will have the light of life."*
>
> John 8:12

In my country, Ukraine, Christmas is the most loved holiday of the year. It has been celebrated in times of peace and in times of war, oppression, terror famines conducted by the evil Soviet empire, and even when Christmas was banned by the state. Those who showed even the slightest signs of remembering the day were persecuted by the Soviets.

My grandfather, a schoolteacher and the son of a priest, refused to become a member of the Communist party. He once told his daughter, my mother, then a kindergartener: "Whatever they tell you, you must remember that there is God in heaven." My mom preserved this secret knowledge throughout the years of her atheist education. When the Soviets were finally gone, she found a church, got baptized, passed her faith on to me, shared the message with her students at the university where she taught, and later went to Kenya to become a full-time missionary.

During the many years of her ministry there, she became disinterested in theological debates. "Whatever, I am a practician!" is her typical response to a theological discussion. There, she can touch Jesus with her hands while wiping, nurturing, and rocking the orphaned baby, embracing an underage single mother, and bringing food and medicine to the sick, aged, neglected, imprisoned, and unloved. There, too, she can see with her physical eyes how Jesus—in the form of the small, meek, and vulnerable—smiles at her in response.

On one of her visits back from Kenya, Mom brought us red-and-black Maasai plaid fabric, which I love to use as a tablecloth during the Christmas season. I consider it my humble way of adding some jazziness to the traditional celebration that usually employs a handmade white embroidered tablecloth, at least on Christmas Eve.

The culture of Advent has come to Ukraine only in recent years. In Ukrainian historical tradition, Christian believers observe not Advent, but the Nativity Fast. It begins on November 28 and lasts until January 6, according to the Gregorian calendar. This time is dedicated to preparing one's heart for Christmas through spiritual disciplines. Prayer and fasting are combined with care for others and almsgiving; abstaining from loud parties and cheerful music is connected with focusing on serving the community; and repentance with forgiveness is emphasized. Traditionally, fasting also involves following a lean diet. On the last day of the Nativity Fast, January 6, we don't eat anything until the first star appears in the sky, to commemorate the hardships of Mary's and Joseph's journey to Bethlehem.

Christmas Eve dinner is called the Holy Supper. It symbolizes Communion, with the whole family gathered around one table (commonly covered by an embroidered tablecloth–or Maasai plaid, in our case). The wax candle is lit. The twelve traditional meals are served—but never as individual portions; the food is placed on the table in painted earthenware dishes to be passed around. There is symbolism in every number, every piece of Christmas decoration, and even in most traditional dishes served on this day.

Among the most beautiful Ukrainian traditions are *Vertep* (a portable nativity scene and play) and caroling. The most famous Ukrainian Christmas song is "Carol of the Bells" ("Shchedryk"), which originated in Western Ukraine and then became known throughout the world in Mykola

Leontovych's arrangement. The English words of the song speak about throwing cares away, joyfulness, and good cheer.

Another Ukrainian carol, one of the most ancient, voices a very different Christmas theme. It is called "Don't Weep, Rachel" and tells the Hebrew scripture story of the second wife of Jacob, the mother of Joseph and Benjamin, from the Book of Jeremiah. Rachel cries for her children in Assyrian captivity. The book of Matthew references Rachel weeping in Ramah for her children murdered by Herod, a reference to Jeremiah 31:15.

In this carol, Rachel is being comforted by the words that this sacrifice is not in vain and that she will receive her children back. Rachel speaks of the fresh ground that has just covered the body of her son.

Even at Christmas, God becomes vulnerable. Love for the world makes God vulnerable, and God's heart is open to the suffering. God chooses not to avert God's gaze. God stays.

PRAY | Almighty, Everlasting, Uncreated God, you became a mortal baby, born from a teenage girl, in a soiled borrowed space in the middle of an oppressed and incapacitated province occupied by an idol-worshiping, bloodthirsty empire. You understand our suffering. Thank you for staying with us. Amen.

REFLECT | How have you experienced the vulnerability, the nearness of God, in your suffering?

LISTEN | "Carol of the Bells" by Eileen, Composer: Shchedryk (by Sharovaari)

God of the Oppressed

READ | Psalm 146:5-10

> *Happy are those whose help is the God of Jacob,*
>> *whose hope is in the LORD their God, . . .*
>> *who executes justice for the oppressed;*
>> *who gives food to the hungry.*
> *The LORD sets the prisoners free.*
>
> Psalm 146:5,7

Jesus, God the vulnerable enfleshed, not only landed in disguise in the "enemy-occupied territory," as C. S. Lewis put it; he did so while choosing the path of *les misérables.*

With the political tensions of the past few years, a discussion has sparked about whether we can technically call Jesus, Joseph, and Mary refugees, or only internally displaced persons. At the time of Jesus' birth, Cleopatra was already dead, and Egypt was not as much a foreign country as a separate province of the Roman Empire. The two provinces, linked by a coastal road called the Way of the Sea, were actually two occupied states. They shared a vast list of cultural differences and lengthy episodes of a common, but not always mutually complementing, history. If our lack of empathy requires the crutches of the legal terms to embrace the contradictory reality of our Savior's earthly days, here are the simple facts: Jesus and his family were fleeing persecution and thus became the asylees in a country that had once enslaved their ancestors. There they found safety, yet no real support.

When the modern-day Herod invaded our country in 2022, my daughter, our dog, and I became refugees in neighboring Poland. Due to the martial law enacted on the first day of the brutal war Russia started against Ukraine, my husband could not leave the country. There was no time to collect our most treasured possessions. After the night that we spent on the floor in the corridor while the sirens were bawling, I hurriedly crammed only the most necessary items into the only suitcase we were taking with us to the evacuation train. Warm clothes, a stack of paper letters, and several books. Among the letters were some from nineteen years ago (the ones my husband wrote to me when we were dating), some from more than half a century ago (that my great-grandfather wrote to his son, my grandfather), and some written recently (from my Mom, while a missionary in Kenya, to my daughter). Our refugee suitcase also contained my dog-eared Bible, my great grandfather's liturgy book published in 1926, and a Ukrainian edition of Tolkien's *The Silmarillion* that I grabbed at the last moment to read aloud to my daughter to keep a semblance of normality in our new refugee life. I also brought Oswald Chamber's *My Utmost for His Highest*. The book had depth and was travel-sized.

Joseph was a carpenter. There must have been a hand-carved cradle, a small gift from Elizabeth, or some jewelry passed to Mary from her mother. We will never know what they left behind. But we know for sure that the three valuable gifts brought to the Holy Family by the magi were God's provision. These potential heirlooms presented to the Savior by the kings became perhaps daily financial support that saved the lives of a refugee family in a foreign country.

The very pragmatism of salvation is embodied in giving up the valuable for the sake of priceless.

PRAY | God of all hope, you are the one who upholds the cause of the oppressed and gives food to the hungry, sets prisoners free, gives sight to the blind, lifts up those who are bowed down, sustains the fatherless and the widowed, and watches over the refugees. Our hope is in you this Advent season. Amen.

REFLECT | If you were forced by war to leave your country quickly, what belongings would you be sure to pack in your bag?

LISTEN | "Don't Cry, Rachel" Composer: Myroslav Skoryk

Strengthen Your Hearts

READ | James 5:7-10

> *Be patient, therefore, brothers and sisters, until the coming of the Lord. The farmer waits for the precious crop from the earth, being patient with it until it receives the early and the late rains. You also must be patient. Strengthen your hearts, for the coming of the Lord is near.*
>
> James 5:7-8

When the war broke out in our country, many well-meaning Christians from around the world came to "visit" us in our suffering, sending prayers and kind advice. We were reminded to be patient and guard or strengthen our hearts. But I wondered, what was it exactly that we were called to guard our hearts against? It was obvious we couldn't guard them against pain or grief. Anger, maybe? Inability to forgive our enemies, at least right away? Without God's grace, it is not possible at all. The long road to reconciliation is one that involves remembering the atrocities and also embodies justice.

Then, against what are we to guard our hearts? While looking at yet another money-raising initiative to help a war-afflicted family on Facebook, I thought that, maybe, instead of trying to guard our hearts from any outward-looking strong emotion, we must make sure that our guarded hearts never grow insensitive to the suffering of God's people around us.

Jesus chose the way of solidarity with people. *Immanuel* means "God with us." Here. In our suffering, pain, and mixed feelings. On Christmas Day, he brought tangible, heavenly love to the world. The kind you can hold, touch, feed, care for, smile at, and cry with—as if it were a baby. For it was.

One of the first English songs I learned as a child from the American missionaries who started coming to Ukraine after the fall of the Iron Curtain was "Jesus Loves Me." Jan, a schoolteacher of many years, taught me how to translate the words of the song into sign language. My favorite motions were nodding yes with my fist and signing the line: "We are weak, but he is strong."

We all are weak and in desperate need of guidance. The crop is yet to be yielded.

PRAY | God of all strength, in the broken world of today, strengthen us against growing callous and blind to those who suffer. We are often weak, but you are strong, in and through us. Amen.

REFLECT | What does the saying "guard your heart" mean to you? In what ways is that guidance helpful and in what ways is it harmful?

LISTEN | "Three Kings" by Menestreli Vocal Group

The Unvarnished Truth

READ | 1 Thessalonians 5:16-24

> *Rejoice always, pray without ceasing, give thanks in all circumstances, for this is the will of God in Christ Jesus for you. Do not quench the Spirit. Do not despise prophecies, but test everything; hold fast to what is good; abstain from every form of evil.*
>
> 1 Thessalonians 5:16-22

It takes guts to face this naked truth: As much as we would like to be the ideal of the always-praying, always-thanking, always-rejoicing Christian, we, as normal humans, are simply unable to do that. It requires the quiet work of the Holy Spirit. Hope is ignited from within, and its conception is never something of our own doing.

As brave as we Ukrainians might look to the world, the reality is that all of us are afraid. Also—sad, frustrated, tired, grumpy, and sick to our stomachs because of this war. Our courage, our message of hope, stems not from the military victories at the front—the "price" of each of them is far too high to greet them with fireworks and dancing—but from that fear that is being stomped on every single day. With every morning breakfast served to the family, every Sunday worship service attended, every donation given, every new book bought, we make the decision to stay—a decision made each and every day.

When you remain actively sensitive to the vulnerable around you—the weak, the weary, the depressed, the wounded—you have no inner resources left for hatred. Ukrainian soldiers often say, "We are not fighting because of hate for our enemies but out of love for our families, our homes, and our land." Hatred might be a mighty fuel, but it runs out soon. Love is the fuel that remains, multiplies, overflows, and roots us in eternity.

Baby Jesus in the hay was staring into his mother's humble, tired, loving eyes and felt at home. The soiled place around him had not been transfigured or renewed, but it was still considered sacred. He was calling his earthly parents, the bewildered and confused couple, to be faithful—not because they were sinless but because they accepted him and focused their lives on his presence. The unvarnished truth stems from the acknowledgment of who we are before the almighty God. God is the one who will take care of the rest.

PRAY | Vulnerable God, we stand before you, just as we are, known and loved by you. We trust you with the outcome of circumstances beyond our control. Amen.

REFLECT | Ponder the truth of the author's statement: "When you remain actively sensitive to the vulnerable around you—the weak, the weary, the depressed, the wounded—you have no inner resources left for hatred." How does this sentiment apply to your life?

LISTEN | "Oh, Come" by Room for More with the Chamber Orchestra "Tarnopil"

Checklists and Prayers

READ | Isaiah 12:2-6

> *Surely God is my salvation;*
> *I will trust and will not be afraid,*
> *for the LORD is my strength and my might;*
> *he has become my salvation.*

Isaiah 12:2

They say that one year of war requires ten years of rebuilding.

Some of my sleepless Ukrainian nights are filled with producing mental checklists of what we, as a nation and as a church, will have to do after the victory. Ramps need to be built everywhere. Shelters and counseling centers formed and sustained. Mountain and seaside retreats for the victims of war created. For there are (and will be) many victims of this war. The facts that there are multitudes and that their suffering is an everyday occurrence do not diminish their individual need for care and healing.

And as I create those checklists in my head, I pray that each of these initiatives would be founded on the realization of the goodness of God and the dignity of each person. I pray that people who lost their limbs, as well as those helping them, know that their disabilities do not make them lose their likeness to the perfect God.

The eternal God did not consider it too humbling to become a newborn, helpless babe. Jesus' torn and crucified body did not become less divine after it was covered with blood, dirt, and scabs. Our wounds and wrinkles, traumas and hurt do not make us less worthy of God's love. From the start, we have never had to earn that love, even when our bodies still carried the scent of the newborn; God offered God's love to us, nonetheless.

God did not make us seek salvation ourselves. God sought us and became our salvation. God did not require that we build up our strength to meet God's expectations; God became our strength.

PRAY | Gracious God, sometimes we are too exhausted and heartbroken to even care about singing. Mental checklists abound. Please be our strength in these moments. Amen.

REFLECT | What are the anxieties that keep you up at night, creating checklists? During your next sleepless night, use the checklist instead as a guide to prayer.

LISTEN | "Silent Night" by Alter Radio

Where the Hurt Is

READ | Luke 3:7-18

And the crowds asked [John], "What, then, should we do?"
In reply he said to them, "Whoever has two coats must share
with anyone who has none, and whoever has food must
do likewise." Even tax collectors came to be baptized, and
they asked him, "Teacher, what should we do?" He said to
them, "Collect no more than the amount prescribed for you."
Soldiers also asked him, "And we, what should we do?" He
said to them, "Do not extort money from anyone by threats
or false accusation, and be satisfied with your wages."

Luke 3:10-14

War, even on the side of justice, means obituaries.

For those far from the frontlines, it means getting up and tending to your responsibilities even when you feel thin and almost nonexistent within. Also, war means the painful, stubborn indestructibility of hope.

I believe that the church should be where the hurt is. To put the thought differently, if the church is not where it hurts, it is godless. If theology does not offer any practical and immediate answers to those who need them most, it is to be dumped at once.

Jesus came in the physical body of a man to put boots (sandals) on the ground of the hurting world, to touch and smell and taste and be present. And to be patient, too. Later on, the church was born, boots on the ground, for the same reason. To be present and be patient, to smell, touch, feel, and cry. To act in love and to believe in reconciliation—and also at the same time to realize that the way to reconciliation is difficult and long.

The sweetness of Christmas is charming, yet most of the celebration in its current form is based on the secular, historical, and cultural roots. The real Christmas is all about uprooting, unearthing (in the most literal meaning of the word), winnowing, and inviting God to plant our hearts once again, this time, in eternity.

Patience in suffering brings joy. Not the shallow, shiny type, of course, but the joy that comes from observing God's faithfulness, day in and day out. The war reality that we, as Ukrainian Christians, are living in has proved to us just that. God is with us.

PRAY | God, you are with us. When the lights go out, you are the one who stays. Amen.

REFLECT | How has the church been a part of your life when you were hurting? When have you seen the church fail to be there at important times?

LISTEN | "The Savior Was Born to Us" by Room for More

Patience in the Waiting

READ | John 11:25-26

Jesus said to her, "I am the resurrection and the life. Those who believe in me, even though they die, will live, and everyone who lives and believes in me will never die. Do you believe this?"

John 11:25-26

Jesus Christ was born to defeat death. In doing so, he took our sorrow, mourning, loneliness, and longing. He took them not just to dissolve them into nothing, but to bear them to the cross and transfigure them into unending joy through his death and resurrection.

After his ascension, he sent us the Holy Spirit to dwell among us. In the Ukrainian language, the word *Comforter* that is attributed to the Holy Spirit, is «Утішитель», with its root coming from the word «утіха», meaning *joy*.

Jesus said, "In the world you face persecution, but take courage: I have conquered the world!" (John 16:33b). He foresaw our suffering. And to make sure that we got through it all and remained faithful, he filled our hearts with a joy of a different kind—the joy of awaiting his victory. That waiting requires patience in the meantime.

Many years ago, I watched an episode in a BBC drama series about World War II. There was a moment in it that I cannot forget. In the drama, the field hospital was located in the forests of France. One of the female volunteers asked her family back home to send her a big box of hyacinth bulbs. She went into the forest, made a small garden, and planted them. When spotted by a nurse, the girl explained: "I just want to have something to look forward to during this winter."

Someday, the winter, the war, and the suffering will end. For now, hope is our small garden of snow-covered hyacinths in the forest by the frontlines.

PRAY | Gracious God, tend our meager garden of hope while we wait on the promise of joy to come. Send us the Comforter to help us make it home. Amen.

REFLECT | What is your version of snow-covered hyacinths? What helps you to wait on God's promise of hope in your life?

LISTEN | "What a Miracle" by Trioda Band

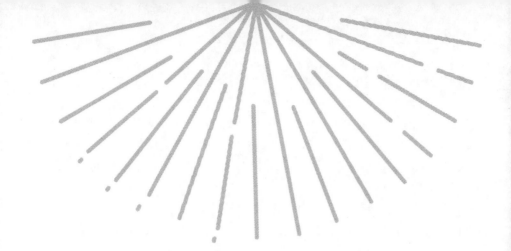

FOURTH WEEK OF ADVENT

Light from South Africa

Love

Sidwell Mokgothu

The South African Celebration of Advent

READ | Revelation 21:22-26

And the city has no need of sun or moon to shine on it, for
the glory of God is its light, and its lamp is the Lamb.

Revelation 21:23

The secular concept of the festive season or the Christian understanding of Advent in South Africa is largely a result of the impact of the migrant labor system in which the Black working class temporarily moved from their poor rural areas to the industrialized cities. This phenomenon was introduced after the discovery of both gold and diamonds in the South African towns of Johannesburg and Kimberley, respectively. Many of the migrant workers would toil in six- or twelve-month contracts that would afford them an opportunity to visit their families in December. The migrants worked the whole year saving money and storing up essentials for their families. They prepared themselves for the great moment of traveling to people who had, for this whole period, been waiting for them. Though this was mostly a historical phenomenon, the pattern that started then, in many ways, remains today.

Like true Advent, this is the time of preparation, anticipation, and hope.

Homegoing in December is still a big phenomenon for many workers and also students in boarding schools and universities. This has helped

South African Christians resonate with and understand the journey of
Joseph and Mary from the town of Nazareth in Galilee to their small
hometown of Bethlehem of Judea. Thus, Advent is mostly a time of home
and family life. Many families organize gatherings to facilitate deep con-
nections. Some of the clans organize events where the different homesteads
introduce themselves to one another. Parents come with their children and
grandchildren to introduce them to one another to build strong familial
bonds over generations. The oldest patriarchs and matriarchs are acknowl-
edged and celebrated as custodians of oral history, heritage, and wisdom.

Advent in South Africa is a time of festivities, music, and the sharing
of food. It is a time when there are all kinds of feasts to mark different rites
of passage in the rural areas and townships. Among some ethnic groups,
it is a time when their boys return from traditional initiation schools, and
feasts are hosted to welcome them. There are also many churches that host
mass baptismal services during the Advent period. The sense of community
is very strong among African people.

Music and food are the central elements of any celebration among
Africans. Music is seen as a gift that God bequeathed to African people.
Africans are known for singing in times of trouble or struggle; and when
they have experienced victory, there is joy. This connection to music finds
expression in the church, with Christmas carols sung to celebrate the antici-
pated birth of Jesus Christ. Central to African feasting is the sharing of
food. It is considered a virtue to be a family that provides hospitality to all
people. In fact, there is an understanding that a home that does not receive
visitors is unfortunate, if not cursed. To receive guests, especially strangers,
is considered a great blessing. Families cook and bake with the expressed
intention of sharing what is made. People go from one house to another to
exchange gifts with neighbors, carrying a plastic bag for the goodies they
receive at different homes.

The African spirituality of *Ubuntu* that advances that human beings
are interdependent has been the bedrock on which life has been lived in
Africa. Seasons like Advent have created space for such spiritual practices
as generosity, hospitality, and celebration to be visibly expressed. Although

this noble heritage has been marred by the so-called modern life that is individualistic, competitive, and selfish, not all is lost. There is hope for the season of Advent to be retrieved and showcased as an opportunity to celebrate the wonderful gift of the Savior born to the world. There are still opportunities for this Christian practice to be integrated with Christian spirituality to make this world a better and joyful place once again.

PRAY | Gracious God, thank you for the supportive structure of family in our lives, whether original or chosen. May we hold these people even closer during this time of the year. Amen.

REFLECT | The African practice of hospitality is unparalleled. How does the expression that "a home that does not receive visitors is unfortunate, if not cursed" speak to you about sharing your home during Advent and Christmas?

LISTEN | "Ndikhokhele Bawo (Lead Me)" by Wits Choir

The Power of the Powerless

READ | Micah 5:2-5a

> *But you, O Bethlehem of Ephrathah,*
> *who are one of the little clans of Judah,*
> *from you shall come forth for me*
> *one who is to rule in Israel,*
> *whose origin is from of old,*
> *from ancient days.*

Micah 5:2

We live in a world dominated by abusive power and authority that is sometimes violent. There are those who are dominant rulers—whether they be individual leaders or certain world nations. It is as if to be powerful, one must exert oppressive power. This has been so throughout all historical epochs of oppression. It was the violent powerful who introduced and practiced slavery. It was mighty nations that went into conquest through the era of colonialism. It was the racist minority regime that subjected the Black majority to the system of apartheid in South Africa. Even today, the world wars of conquest are about empires lording their power over others and subjecting them to suffering.

The same situation faced Israel, as Micah reports in our scripture reading. Israel was surrounded by powerful Assyria, where the prophet viewed the nation to be under siege. During that challenging context, Micah pointed to the possibility of a promised ruler. Israel had lived for a long time with the promise and expectation of a Messiah who would deliver and rescue the nation. For years, Israel's prophets and psalmists foretold the people of the viceroy who would represent God's rule on earth. Yahweh's anointed one would descend from the house of David, restore Israel, and establish the expected kingdom.

It is this expectation and hope that provided Israel with its resilience and staying power during difficult situations. It is this redemptive hope that we should hold on to: the Lord will always come into whatever situation we find ourselves.

Micah offers a prophetic word that is countercultural and contradictory to the dominant practice in the world. Whereas Israel would need to have power enough to defend itself, the prophet points to soft power for the nation. Whereas the dominant view is that help would come from the more established powerful clans or tribes of Israel, the prophet points out that it would come from Bethlehem of Ephrathah, which was the smallest of the clans. Micah models to us what can be considered as the power of powerlessness. This is a spirituality that does not rely on the use of powerful weaponry that is meant to destroy those who are opposing us. It is the kind of power that is reliant on the external power of God that is accessed by tapping into the inner soul.

Micah's countercultural prophetic message is that this anointed ruler is one who will stand not in his own power but in the strength of the Lord derived from the majesty of the name of God.

Advent presents to us that similar faith and hope that Micah advocates. Advent is a time of deep hope for peace, found in surrender and reliance on God. Advent reminds us that, in whatever oppressive situations we find ourselves, we should wait and hope for Christ, who shall come to deliver and save us. Christ's rescue mission is not based on violent vengefulness but on grace.

Advent reminds those who are followers of Christ that, in this world where the powerful lord it over the oppressed, the poor, and the marginalized through unjust systems and structures, the anointed son of God will come forth to them too. Advent must assure those who are weak and vulnerable that in Christ "they shall live secure" (Mic. 5:4) and that Christ will be great to them to the ends of the earth.

PRAY | God of the powerless, restore our hope that you will come through for us too. We are never alone and we are never without the power of your grace. Amen.

REFLECT | In what situations of powerlessness in our world would you like to see the strength of God's grace realized?

LISTEN | "An African Christmas" by Drakensberg Boys Choir

Song of Victory

READ | Luke 1:46-55

> *"My soul magnifies the Lord,*
> *and my spirit rejoices in God my Savior,*
> *for he has looked with favor on the lowly state of his servant.*
> *Surely from now on all generations will call me blessed."*
> Luke 1:46b-48

The Bible has several women who led songs to express their worship to God. Miriam, the sister of Aaron and Moses, took a timbrel and invited women to join in a song of victory after the Israelites passed the Red Sea (see Exodus 15:2-21). Hannah, the mother of Samuel burst into a song of victory that she attributed to God, even in her barrenness (see 1 Samuel 2:1-10). Mary, the mother of Jesus Christ, also could evoke the Hebrew spirituality of celebrating through song, even in dire situations. It is interesting that these three women all reflected on the liberative nature of the Lord. They burst into song and declared their joy, even in the midst of the challenges they faced. Their songs carry spirituality that should be evoked during our times of challenges.

The Christian season of Advent is a time of great worship celebration through song. It wasn't just the shepherds who were able to sing in the dark night, but Mary was too. Mary's song has provided many people and women, particularly those in distress, direction on how to live with hope and expectation.

"The Magnificat" is a song of victory that Mary sings immediately after the annunciation—the great announcement from the angel Gabriel. This announcement was more like a promissory note: it was a promise about what would happen in the future. All those things have not yet happened, but Mary burst into song. It is a song full of conviction and faith. She trusts and believes in the faithfulness of God, even before the events manifest.

While the great announcement was about elevating Mary and putting her at the center of God's salvation plan, she takes the focus away from herself and recognizes that she is a mere servant. She instead uses worship to help herself remember that God is in the midst of what is happening. Her song chooses to praise and magnify God as the main character and subject of salvation. It is God who is worthy of celebration and praise.

In a selfish world where the period of Advent and Christmas is so commercialized and the culture is more consumerist, the focus of Mary's song is a form of prophetic protest and a liberation song. Like Mary, we must commit our souls and spirits to the Lord. Throughout the song, God is described and affirmed in a way that is more meaningful to the one who knows suffering and struggle against powers and principalities. Each one of us has to acknowledge, affirm, and celebrate God in the manner in which we have come to experience and know God. To those of us who are left exposed and vulnerable in one way or another, we identify with Mary in acknowledging the Lord as mighty. To those whose lives are shattered or needing to be rescued, God is the Savior.

The content of Mary's song is a radical gospel: power, especially when it is not used for the wellbeing of the people, will not last long. God brings "down the powerful from their thrones." We live in a world of rising inequality, where the gap between the minority who are super rich and the masses who are acutely poor is increasing. Those who are rich from their exploitation of the lowly do not find favor with God and are instead rejected and sent away.

While to some, Advent is a time of festivities, it is also a time where the poverty and destitution of others is seriously exposed. Although the world discriminates and excludes those who are lowly and needy, God feeds the many who are hungry and provides them with "good things."

PRAY | Liberating God, we pray that all of your people, in whatever circumstances they find themselves, may find their own song of victory in this time of Advent. Amen.

REFLECT | In the face of challenging circumstances, what is your "go-to" song, one that refocuses you on God's faithfulness in your life?

LISTEN | "African Christmas—The Sun Shines Down" by Frits365

Woman-to-Woman Affirmation

READ | Luke 1:39-45

> *And Elizabeth was filled with the Holy Spirit and exclaimed*
> *with a loud cry, "Blessed are you among women, and*
> *blessed is the fruit of your womb. . . . And blessed is she*
> *who believed that there would be a fulfillment of what was*
> *spoken to her by the Lord."*
>
> Luke 1:41b-42, 45

The challenges of discrimination and abuse that women face around the world and in its institutions find expression even in the church. There is a continuum of theological positions of different churches and related experiences of women in the ministry of these churches. Women ministers across denominations usually experience some form of patriarchy and abuse within congregations. This powerful system has socialized men to believe that they are better and more gifted than women. Church structures are used to deny and exclude women from meaningful roles. Sometimes this is done publicly, and at times, it is done privately and subtly.

The story and roles of Mary, the mother of Jesus Christ, and her cousin, Elizabeth, the mother of John the Baptist, are a powerful testimony to the healing and encouragement of women, whatever their roles. God chooses these two women to play a role in the salvation of the world. They serve as liberating models for many women, showing that God does love women and affirms them for God's ministry and mission. The two women had the privilege of being visited by the angel Gabriel, who shared the good news of the imminent birth of two sons, for whom God had a purpose and a mission.

Elizabeth was the first who had received the unbelievable message in her old age. Luke reports that both Elizabeth and her husband, Zechariah, were from the priestly lineages: Zechariah was from the lineage Abijah, and Elizabeth was a descendant of Aaron. The angel brings them into this joint ministry and announces to Zechariah that Elizabeth will bear a son and not to be afraid.

Mary also had the privilege of the visitation from the angel Gabriel. Mary was, by Hebrew cultural standards, a marginalized and vulnerable person with few rights. She was a young virgin from the rural town of Nazareth of Galilee. She was a newly betrothed woman with little social standing. Despite her social and cultural standing, Mary received powerful words of affirmation that would be good news to all women who are struggling to live their life purpose in a patriarchal society.

The encounters with Gabriel prepared the two women to meet for mutual support and celebration of the affirmations they had received. Mary, pregnant with the Savior of the world, goes on an intentional journey to seek Elizabeth to affirm her.

Advent is a time of great affirmation for all those who doubt their role and contribution in the ministry and mission of Christ, especially women. The role of women should not be a threat to any male servant of the Lord. There is so much to be done together.

PRAY | Loving and affirming God, thank you for equipping and encouraging all who are called. Thank you especially for the power and presence of women leaders in the church and the world. Amen.

REFLECT | Elizabeth's and Mary's relationship models the beauty of collaboration and mutual affirmation. With whom do you have a spiritual friendship of mutual encouragement? Give thanks for that person today.

LISTEN | "Tshedza Tshanga (My Light)" by Maduvha

The Great Escape

READ | Matthew 2:13-25

> *Now after they had left, an angel of the Lord appeared to Joseph in a dream and said, "Get up, take the child and his mother, and flee to Egypt, and remain there until I tell you, for Herod is about to search for the child, to destroy him." Then Joseph got up, took the child and his mother by night, and went to Egypt and remained there until the death of Herod.*
>
> Matthew 2:13-15a

We live in a world that is violent and threatening to the most vulnerable, including children. There are many parts of the world where children are under threat from the powerful. Many of God's people live in situations of distress, oppression, and exploitation. Whereas Advent and Christmas have been commercialized and made to promote splashy material things, the season is a time of hope and joy anchored in simplicity for many who are suffering.

The innocent and unknown baby born in a peripheral manger in the rural village of Bethlehem posed a serious threat to King Herod. The arrival of three wise men who had followed a strange miraculous star from the east unsettled and made the powerful king vulnerable and fearful. The simple act of celebrating the baby, paying homage and presenting him with birthday gifts, became a serious threat to the established kingdom of Herod.

This led Herod to scheme and hatch an evil plan to kill and destroy the baby Jesus. The threat was so serious that Herod was prepared to mobilize his powerful system and structures to hunt and kill all other newly-born children as collateral damage (see Matthew 2:16).

Like many refugees scattered all over the world, Joseph and Mary became displaced from the safety of their homeland. Many men, women, and children have fled from their homes to escape the harsh destructive wars and sociopolitical and economic situations in their countries of birth. They are pursuing their dreams of a better life somewhere else.

The United Nations High Commissioner for Refugees, the International Organization for Migration, Amnesty International, and other world multilateral bodies report on the numbers of peoples of the world who have taken risks to escape from their African and Middle Eastern home countries, fleeing to countries in the West. They view their own places of birth as hell because of the violent conflict, sexual abuse, persecution, extortion, and poverty they experience. They are prepared to undertake the arduous journeys through the perilous Mediterranean Sea. Although the prospect of death is evident to them, they are prepared to face that danger compared to the harsh oppression and exploitation at the hands of the powerful kinsmen. Even if they were to be taken to prison in Europe, they view prison as relative heaven with great possibilities of life compared to the trauma at home. Thousands have drowned and perished in the Mediterranean Sea. Many have fallen victim to human trafficking, where they are sold as modern slaves in foreign countries. They are kept and exploited to serve the powerful and the rich without any human rights or protection.

The good news of Advent and Christmas is about the great escape of salvation. It is about the rescuing of people—not of statistics, as migrants, refugees, and asylum seekers have come to be thought of—and the dreams and hopes of individuals, families, communities, and sometimes nations. Christians worship and follow the God who is not oppressively powerful but who, in the baby Jesus, escaped into exile and became a refugee in Africa. This season celebrates the Christ, who together with his parents, found safety and security in a foreign land.

Advent and Christmas speak to the importance of Christian solidarity with the many who are vulnerable and marginalized. Providing love, care, and support to those who have escaped the harsh and traumatic realities of their home countries to seek life is the act of welcoming the Christ child into our midst, affirmed in Jesus' words to his disciples in Matthew 25:40: "Truly I tell you, just as you did it to one of the least of these . . . you did it to me."

The truth of Christmas is that there is nothing in this world, irrespective of its power, that is going to stop God's salvation plan. God's determination to set free and usher salvation is unstoppable. Evil and darkness do not overpower good and light forever. Powerful and oppressive systems do not remain forever.

PRAY | Saving God, we pray for all of those who are in situations of exile. May your goodness and light prevail in governmental systems and through dedicated people to rescue them. Amen.

REFLECT | What is one small action you can take this Advent to show Christian solidarity with refugees seeking safety in your country?

LISTEN | "Tshepa Thapelo (Trust in Prayer)" by Soweto Gospel Choir

The Prince of Peace

READ | Isaiah 9:1-7

> *For a child has been born for us,*
> *a son given to us;*
> *authority rests upon his shoulders,*
> *and he is named*
> *Wonderful Counselor, Mighty God,*
> *Everlasting Father, Prince of Peace.*
>
> Isaiah 9:6

Our present context, just like that of Isaiah and at the birth of Christ, is often characterized by the absence of peace. All these contexts are marked by high levels of violence that manifest in different ways. Isaiah's context was that of the prophecy of war and destruction, darkness and gloom described in chapter 8.

The socio-cultural and politico-economic context into which Christ was born was violent and oppressive. Israel was under colonial rule by the Roman Empire under the leadership of Emperor Caesar. This emperor used taxes to exploit the poor nation.

Nations and communities the world over have experienced colonial occupation. Whereas colonial rule has ended in many countries on the African continent, other forms of neo-colonial economic exploitation of many countries continue. Many powerful Western countries sponsor military coups and dictatorships to extract mineral and energy resources from these countries or to support their military-industrial complex. This is the powerful world industry that manufactures lethal military technologies. They sustain their business by instigating wars in different parts of the world.

Violence has become the prominent language that human beings have come to embrace. This manifests in macro systems that involve powerful nations of the world as well as in local communities. It manifests in the form of patriarchy and misogyny through gender-based violence and femicide where women are raped and killed in large numbers.

In this scripture, we receive the promise of a different kind of ruler, whose birth ushers in a countercultural system that contradicts the status quo. In a world that relies on violence to rule and subjugate others, we are promised a young Prince of Peace whose reign is different: "Great will be his authority, and there shall be endless peace" (Isa. 9:7).

Whereas we are used to violent governments that lord it over the weak, Christ's authority is one that shall grow continually in peace. Advent and Christmas are about this Prince, who brings to us the Hebrew understanding of *shalom*. This is the kind of peace in which perpetrators of conflict or violence make right what they have taken or stolen. Shalom is the sense of peace that leaves the aggrieved fully restored. It is this peace that resides in the soul and wells up to be shared with others.

PRAY | God of peace, we pray for true shalom in our world—true and genuine peace that is grounded in righteousness and justice. May we do our part to bring about this kind of peace. Amen.

REFLECT | In some churches, "the passing of the peace" is a regular part of the worship service; people greet one another with these words: "The peace of the Lord be with you." In addition to saying these words aloud at church, how can you incorporate them into your intercessory prayer for others?

LISTEN | "Christmas in Cape Town" by New Apostolic Young People's Choir

The Ever-Present God

READ | Matthew 1:18-25

> *"Look, the virgin shall become pregnant and give birth to a son,
> and they shall name him Emmanuel," which means,
> "God is with us."*
>
> Matthew 1:23

N ames are important in the Hebrew language. Many of the names carried some sacred spiritual meaning:

* Abraham—the father of many
* Isaiah—salvation of the Lord
* Jeremiah—God will exalt
* Jesus—God is salvation
* Christ or Messiah—the anointed one

Names were given not because they sounded nice or belonged to some celebrity. They described situations in which people found themselves. They also declared the wish and hope of the people who gave them. They captured the desires of the parents for what the child would be or do. Those who received such names attempted to or committed to living up to their names.

In today's scripture, the book of Matthew reports the good news of the fulfillment of the promise that Isaiah prophesied to King Ahaz of Judah centuries before. The young virgin is no more just a descriptive abstract but has an identity. The expected boy has been born to the young woman, Mary.

Ours is a God who does not abandon God's people. Immanuel is, in Jesus Christ, more than just a name. It is the affirmation of God who is still living among the people. Advent and Christmas remind us of the God who does not leave nor forsake us. We are assured of the God who identifies with us. At Christmas, we hear the powerful words of Isaac Watts' song written in 1719:

> *Joy to the World, the Lord is come!*
> *Let earth receive her King;*
> *Let every heart prepare Him room,*
> *And heaven and nature sing . . .*

The Lord Jesus Christ is the joy that comes to the world. All we must do is to receive him.

The Immanuel God is one who reminds Israel of the Exodus God. The God reported in Exodus who had the compassionate capacity to observe the misery of the people, hear their cries, know their sufferings, and deliver them, is the same God who, in Jesus, is incarnate and dwells with us. This is the God who sent their ancestors the *Shekhinah*—a sign of assurance of God's presence through the pillars of cloud and fire during the day and night. This is the God who showed up to provide them with manna in the wilderness (see Exodus 16:4-5), who showed up in Nebuchadnezzar's fiery furnace and became the fourth person (see Daniel 3:19-25). This is the omnipresent God of whom the psalmist commented, "If I ascend to heaven, you are there; if I make my bed in Sheol, you are there" (Ps. 139:8).

Immanuel—the manifestation of God with us—is good news in a world that experiences the absence of those who are supposed to be custodians of life-giving hope among the people. Immanuel is the antithesis of public leaders who are absent and are nowhere to be seen among the people that they are to serve.

In situations of helplessness and hopelessness, Advent and Christmas usher in the assurance of the God who is present. In Christ, God becomes available and accessible to the poor and marginalized of the world. It was this gospel that led the late Archbishop Desmond Tutu to echo the words of the apostle Paul to the oppressed and struggling Black people of apartheid South Africa: "What then are we to say about these things? If God is for us, who is against us?" (Rom. 8:31).

PRAY | Ever-present God, help us to remember, in good times and bad, that you are with us and you are *for* us. Amen.

REFLECT | What moments of God-with-you can you recall in these past weeks of Advent? Write each of them, with a short note about the experience.

LISTEN | "Emmanuel" by Solly Mahlangu

Guide for Small Groups

Follow this outline for four one-hour gatherings during the season of Advent. Group meetings can be led by a designated leader, or leadership could be rotated among members of the group each week. Gather in a comfortable place and, if possible, have group members form a circle.

Week One

GATHER (5 minutes)

Light a candle. Pray together, using one of the following options:

* Pray extemporaneously, asking God to open the minds and hearts of those gathered and lead to new moments of discovery.
* Speak in unison a written prayer.
* Allow each person who desires to contribute a sentence or two of prayer.
* Hold a few moments for silent prayer.

PREPARE (10 minutes)

* What experiences have shaped your expectations or made you aware of God's guidance this week?
* Which devotion from this week's readings spoke to you in an especially noteworthy way, and in what ways did it do so?

LISTEN (10 minutes)

Play one of the musical selections from the week or ask for suggestions as to which song to play.

* Where did you hear God speaking through the musical selections this week?
* How were you challenged by the musical selections this week?
* What insights did the music give you into the author's culture and experience of Advent?

LEARN (10 minutes)

Ask someone to read aloud Matthew 1:18-25.

* What is comforting and familiar about the story of Christ's birth?
* What is challenging about this part of the story of Christ's birth?
* What is something new you are hearing or exploring this year as you prepare for Christ's birth?

REFLECT (20 minutes)

Use the following questions in a time of engagement with the group, focusing on hearing and understanding the insight of your fellow group members.

* What does "Advent" mean to you?
* What was your experience of Advent growing up?

* What hopes do you have for your community? For the world?
* What is your definition of *peace*? How can you join God's work to bring peace to earth?
* To what work is God inviting you through the birth of the Christ child this Advent season?

Use these questions from the end of each day's meditation for further conversation and reflection.

* Day One: Who were the people whose light shone on your life and gave you warmth? How did the light of God keep you going this far?
* Day Two: How are you making a point of finding joy in your life during Advent? What in your life makes happiness "the proof of the nine"?
* Day Three: Today, what are your deepest forms of hope? What prayers of restoration do you need to pray today?
* Day Four: What people or groups of people in your life have laid a foundation of love for you in such a way as to allow you to be able to experience Advent love more fully?
* Day Five: Is the idea that "God so loved" all the earth a new perspective for you? How can you join your love for a certain part of creation with God's love through action?
* Day Six: What if to love God is to love animals? Where do you see this kind of love in your life?
* Day Seven: In that ways can you learn to love God in more expansive ways? Are you awake and ready for these challenges again this Advent?

GO (5 minutes)

Share prayer concerns among the group and close your meeting with a prayer.

Week Two

GATHER (5 minutes)

Light a candle. Pray together, using one of the following options:

* Pray extemporaneously, asking God to open the minds and hearts of those gathered and lead to new moments of discovery.
* Speak in unison a written prayer.
* Allow each person who desires to contribute a sentence or two of prayer.
* Hold a few moments for silent prayer.

PREPARE (10 minutes)

* What experiences have shaped your expectations or made you aware of God's guidance this week?
* Which devotion from this week's readings spoke to you in an especially noteworthy way, and in what ways did it do so?

LISTEN (10 minutes)

Play one of the musical selections from the week or ask for suggestions as to which song to play.

* Where did you hear God speaking through the musical selections this week?
* How were you challenged by the musical selections this week?
* What insights did the music give you into the author's culture and experience of Advent?

LEARN (10 minutes)

Ask someone to read aloud Matthew 2:1-12.

* What is comforting and familiar about the story of Christ's birth?
* What is challenging about this part of the story of Christ's birth?
* What is something new you are hearing or exploring this year as you prepare for Christ's birth?

REFLECT (20 minutes)

Use the following questions in a time of engagement with the group, focusing on hearing and understanding the insight of your fellow group members.

* How does the way our culture celebrates Christmas affect your honoring of Advent and Christmas?
* What experiences and practices make Advent and Christmas different from other times of the year for you?
* What about the story of Christ's birth is radical for our world right now?
* What spiritual darkness are you experiencing?
* The author says, "Advent is not simply preparation for Christmas. Instead, we are making ourselves ready to meet Christ in the most unexpected people." Beyond Christmas, what do you feel the season of Advent prepares you for?

Use these questions from the end of each day's meditation for further conversation and reflection.

* Day One: What practice from another church or denomination could you try this Advent to bring new life to your experience?
* Day Two: In what ways have you believed in a "sugar-coated story devoid of political and social implications"? How does a clear reading of the Gospels change that perspective?

* Day Three: Where do you see glimpses of God's new creation coming to pass around you?

* Day Four: How do you understand your baptism as a subversive act?

* Day Five: What ponderings do you have in response to the Madeleine L'Engle quote: "Maybe you have to know the darkness before you can appreciate the light." How have you experienced this in your life?

* Day Six: The author writes, "The barometer of a nation's righteousness is how it treats the most vulnerable in its midst." How do you rate your country's righteousness against this statement? What is your prayer for your country in this regard?

* Day Seven: When the gospel is used to justify marginalization, discrimination, bigotry, and hatred toward the other, our hope diminishes and our Advent light dims. What acts brighten the light of Advent?

GO (5 minutes)

Share prayer concerns among the group and close your meeting with a prayer.

Week Three

GATHER (5 minutes)

Light a candle. Pray together, using one of the following options:

* Pray extemporaneously, asking God to open the minds and hearts of those gathered and lead to new moments of discovery.
* Speak in unison a written prayer.
* Allow each person who desires to contribute a sentence or two of prayer.
* Hold a few moments for silent prayer.

PREPARE (10 minutes)

* What experiences have shaped your expectations or made you aware of God's guidance this week?
* Which devotion from this week's readings spoke to you in an especially noteworthy way, and in what ways did it do so?

LISTEN (10 minutes)

Play one of the musical selections from the week or ask for suggestions as to which song to play.

* Where did you hear God speaking through the musical selections this week?
* How were you challenged by the musical selections this week?
* What insights did the music give you into the author's culture and experience of Advent?

LEARN (10 minutes)

Ask someone to read aloud Matthew 2:13-18.

 * What is comforting and familiar about the story of Christ's birth?
 * What is challenging about this part of the story of Christ's birth?
 * What is something new you are hearing or exploring this year as you prepare for Christ's birth?

REFLECT (20 minutes)

Use the following questions in a time of engagement with the group, focusing on hearing and understanding the insight of your fellow group members.

 * What challenges to your faith have you experienced? What challenges have generations before you experienced?
 * How do the political realities of Christ's birth affect your understanding of the Christmas story today?
 * In what ways are you motivated by hate? How are you motivated by love?
 * Where is the hurt in your community? How is the church showing up there? How are you showing up there?

Use these questions from the end of each day's meditation for further conversation and reflection.

 * Day One: How have you experienced the vulnerability, the nearness of God, in your suffering?
 * Day Two: If you were forced by war to leave your country quickly, what belongings would you be sure to pack in your bag?
 * Day Three: What does the saying "guard your heart" mean to you? In what ways is that guidance helpful and in what ways is it harmful?

* Day Four: Ponder the truth of the author's statement: "When you remain actively sensitive to the vulnerable around you—the weak, the weary, the depressed, the wounded—you have no inner resources left for hatred." How does this sentiment apply to your life?
* Day Five: What are the anxieties that keep you up at night, creating checklists?
* Day Six: How has the church been a part of your life when you were hurting? When have you seen the church fail to be there at important times?
* Day Seven: What is your version of snow-covered hyacinths? What helps you to wait on God's promise of hope in your life?

GO (5 minutes)

Share prayer concerns among the group and close your meeting with a prayer.

Week Four

GATHER (5 minutes)

Light a candle. Pray together, using one of the following options:

* Pray extemporaneously, asking God to open the minds and hearts of those gathered and lead to new moments of discovery.
* Speak in unison a written prayer.
* Allow each person who desires to contribute a sentence or two of prayer.
* Hold a few moments for silent prayer.

PREPARE (10 minutes)

* What experiences have shaped your expectations or made you aware of God's guidance this week?
* Which devotion from this week's readings spoke to you in an especially noteworthy way, and in what ways did it do so?

LISTEN (10 minutes)

Play one of the musical selections from the week or ask for suggestions as to which song to play.

* Where did you hear God speaking through the musical selections this week?
* How were you challenged by the musical selections this week?
* What insights did the music give you into the author's culture and experience of Advent?

LEARN (10 minutes)

Ask someone to read aloud Matthew 2:18-23.

* What is comforting and familiar about the story of Christ's birth?
* What is challenging about this part of the story of Christ's birth?
* What is something new you are hearing or exploring this year as you prepare for Christ's birth?

REFLECT (20 minutes)

Use the following questions in a time of engagement with the group, focusing on hearing and understanding the insight of your fellow group members.

* What traveling do you traditionally do around Christmas, or are you planning to do this year? How does traveling shape your experience of the holiday?
* What promises do you believe God will faithfully fulfill?
* Whose "role and contribution in the ministry and mission of Christ" do you particularly appreciate? How have you shown them appreciation?
* What does it mean to be an agent of God's peace? How are you an agent for peace?
* In what ways is Christ present in the world today?

Use these questions from the end of each day's meditation for further conversation and reflection.

* Day One: The African practice of hospitality is unparalleled. How does the expression that "a home that does not receive visitors is unfortunate, if not cursed" speak to you about sharing your home during Advent and Christmas?
* Day Two: In what situations of powerlessness in our world would you like to see the strength of God's grace realized?

* Day Three: In the face of challenging circumstances, what is your "go-to" song, one that refocuses you on God's faithfulness in your life?

* Day Four: Elizabeth's and Mary's relationship models the beauty of collaboration and mutual affirmation. With whom do you have a spiritual friendship of mutual encouragement?

* Day Five: What is one small action you can take this Advent to show Christian solidarity with refugees seeking safety in your country?

* Day Six: In some churches, "the passing of the peace" is a regular part of the worship service in which people greet one another with these words: "The peace of the Lord be with you." In addition to saying these words aloud at church, how can you incorporate them into your intercessory prayer for others?

* Day Seven: What moments of God-with-you can you recall in these past weeks of Advent?

GO (5 minutes)

Share prayer concerns among the group and close your meeting with a prayer.